HERDING WORDS

HERDING WORDS

A Brand Copywriter's Guide

DAVID R. WOODRUFF

Published by Wheatmark®

Herding Words: A Brand Copywriter's Guide

Copyright © 2019 David R. Woodruff. All rights reserved. No part of this book may be reproduced or retransmitted in any form or by any means without the written permission of the publisher.

Published by Wheatmark®
2030 E. Speedway Boulevard Suite 106
Tucson, Arizona 85719 USA
www.wheatmark.com

ISBN: 978-1-62787-697-1 (paperback)
ISBN: 978-1-62787-688-9 (ebook)

LCCN: 2019937668

The title of this book is no accident. Whenever I embark on a new writing assignment, I immediately imagine a corral of all the hundreds or thousands of words I may consider using. Then I anticipate the challenge of herding each of them, one at a time, into a careful arrangement—ensuring that each serves a unique and purposeful role.

~ David R. Woodruff

Also by David R. Woodruff

From Dad, with Love: Everyday Wisdom for Young Adults

Copyright ® 2016

CONTENTS

Preface   **xiii**
    A little bit about me xiv
    And the credit goes to … xv

Introduction   **xvii**

PART 1: THE TRUTH ABOUT HEADLINES   **1**
    Getting to the desired action 3

PART 2: CONSTRUCTING BODY COPY   **9**
    Research. Then research some more. 12
    A copywriter's role as mediator 13
    The story arc 14
    The role of subheads 15
    Pull quotes 16
    Get personal with your narrative 17

PART 3: THE CALL TO ACTION   **21**
    Don't be coy 24
    CTAs: Here, there, everywhere 24
    May I have another? 25

PART 4: COPYEDITING   **29**
    The 80 percent push 32
    Shelf it 33
    Negotiating copyedits 34
    Know your style guide 36
    Keep your SEO in check 37
    A welcome ally 39

PART 5: EMAIL SUBJECT LINES — 41
What makes a good email subject line? 44
Testing, testing … 45

PART 6: BLOGGING — 47
Build industry thought leadership and your brand 50

PART 7: WRITING FOR THE WEB — 53
The dynamism of web content 56
Length 57
Tone 57
SEO 58
Internet matchmaking 58

PART 8: CUSTOMER PERSONAS — 59
What is a persona? 62
What you need to know about your persona 63
Where to get the data 64
Sample B2B persona 66
Messages for Perl 67
Your customer persona as a good friend 68

PART 9: WRITING FOR SOCIAL MEDIA — 71
The swiping struggle is real 74
Great content doesn't share itself 75
Messaging tips for the social media–minded 76

PART 10: COPY THAT EMOTES — 79
It's all about them (not you) 82
Yeah, but why? 82
Make 'em feel something, then
make 'em do something 84
High emotion words 84

PART 11: A TINY WORD ON MICROCOPY   **87**
   The what-to-do-now copy 91

PART 12: GOING DEEP   **93**
   What's in a word? 95
   Know your process 97

A Final Word on Words   **101**
   Get your head around it 101
   Clients and accountants and copywriters—oh my .. 101

PREFACE

I am a fortunate guy. I have had, and continue to have, the pleasure of doing what I love most in my work—and that is writing. For decades, it seems I've crossed over so many rites of passage as a creative professional. Just when I think I've learned all there is to know about brand copywriting or marketing in general, the world and the infinite sentiments it inspires (environmental, technological, political, or sociological) shift yet again, offering a whole new set of conditions that challenge my knowledge and prod me from my comfort zone to learn and adapt. These shifts have become the pillars of my professional and personal growth. And I have come to rely on them to help me and my craft evolve.

But the one thing that remains a constant in my work is my philosophy behind the writing. Call it a mind-set or method influenced by personal bias; either way, it has become foundational to my approach to copywriting—and that approach allows me to create and express without boundaries, and remain true to myself in my work.

This philosophy serves as the very essence of this book.

I wrote this book as a professional development guide for marketing copywriters, brand managers, content developers, or anyone responsible for crafting brand narrative. Based on my experience, observations, and willingness to try new and different messaging techniques, it's designed to help elevate a writer's insight and expertise as a brand storyteller. But more so, to inspire them to go beyond topical features and benefits and get to the core truth about a brand's promise—then transform those insights into a powerful narrative for print, digital, and web marketing communications.

A little bit about me

I am an award-winning content writer and precision editor with more than two decades of experience developing strategic brand messaging for B2B and B2C print, digital, and web marketing communications. My work has been recognized by MarCom Awards, one of the most respected creative competitions in the world that honors excellence in marketing communications. I earned several platinum and two gold awards for print marketing assets, including a corporate magazine cover/feature story.

Central to my success is my passion for diving deep into a brand's promise. I enjoy collaborating with subject matter experts, industry consultants, and senior-level management across organizations to identify brand, marketing, and sales objectives for increasing revenue—then working closely with creative teams to develop marketing assets that align with achieving those objectives.

Earlier in my career, I owned and operated a niche Marcom agency that delivered strategic brand copywriting and editing for small to large organizations. I never knew that my decision to earn a bachelor of science degree in business would ultimately serve me so well during my agency years and beyond, but it provided some critical perspective around the business value of strategic messaging. Today, I devote much of my time and talent supporting in-house corporate creative teams and working closely with brand managers, art directors, graphic designers, and other writers to help elevate the value of a brand through content development.

After a decade of earnest study, I was certified as having advanced-level proficiency in Spanish by the American Council on the Teaching of Foreign Languages (ACTFL) via the University of California San Diego. Every now and then, I'm honored with an opportunity to write or edit marketing content for Spanish-speaking markets, with the grateful support of native speakers who help keep my content messaging on true north.

My industry experience includes technology, telecommunications, healthcare, manufacturing, financial services, life sciences, retail, mortgage, automotive, government, insurance, media and entertainment, and transportation technology. Despite the exhaustive list, I'm confident that my industry exposure will continue to expand as I continue saying yes to new and exciting brand messaging opportunities.

And the credit goes to …

All that being said, I didn't get to where I am today alone. Not by a long shot.

In fact, this book would not be possible—nor could I be the copywriter I am today—if not for the many writers, designers, brand managers, and other highly creative professionals with whom I've collaborated, shared interesting and unique concepts, and held spirited messaging debates over the course of my career. Though expressed through my own learning and experience, this book reflects the collective wisdom that continues to forge the indelible wake of my experience as a career copywriter.

I wish to thank each and every amazingly talented

marketing professional with whom I've had the pleasure of creating great content over the years (you know who you are). I also wish to give a special thanks to Andrea Stamas, a talented brand manager, for her keen editorial insights during the initial drafting of this book. Her input, along with the editorial expertise of the publisher, is a testament that collaboration is the finest ingredient for procuring premium content.

This book is dedicated to you, the reader, and the next generation of brand storytellers.

INTRODUCTION
LEAD WITH AUTHENTICITY

You're a marketing copywriter. More than that, you're a creative professional. That means people—your clients, customers, and prospects—expect something powerfully different from you, something that only you are uniquely skilled to deliver. And, surprise! They want more than words.

They want a story.

In no other time in history has the consumer marketplace been so intensely competitive. This reality is compounded by the explosion of a digital economy that has completely transformed the way companies communicate their brand messages—and the way people consume them.

Enter you.

> While it takes a marketing village to successfully launch and evolve a brand, you can be sure that behind every creative tribe is at least one voice—a skilled, talented, and highly intuitive storyteller who gets it.
>
> **Behind every creative tribe is a skilled storyteller.**

That is, they get the fundamental *thing* that's capable of unlocking brand value with every carefully chosen, precisely executed word. Like an epic novel, they orchestrate and conduct an ongoing brand story that reaches across a vast multichannel horizon that's so genuine, sincere, and yes, gripping, that audiences dare not miss a chapter.

So, what is this *thing*? In a word, authenticity.

And that's what this book is about. It's about truth in storytelling—and your role as a copywriter in transforming a brand message from a well-intended grouping of words into a truly relatable, relevant, and meaningful dialogue that your audience genuinely wants to engage in at every stage of the customer journey. And why? Because the message is grounded in raw, unabashed authenticity. It is purposeful messaging that tethers every word and sentiment to truth—the truth about what the brand delivers, and what it doesn't.

That's your job.

Consumer tolerance for clutter—baseless product pitches, poor or mistimed messaging, fluff marketing speak, you name it—has all but flatlined. Tired and frustrated with empty words, they have little time to waste on filtering "marketing vapor" to get to a brand's truth. And the fact is, if you won't tell them what they need to know about your brand up front—in a simple, honest, and informative way—there are dozens or even hundreds of competitors who'll be happy to step up.

Whether you're a copywriter, brand manager, content developer, or any creative professional tasked with crafting or editing strategic brand messaging for print, digital, or web marketing communications, it's your job to get them there—to the truth. This book is designed to help you embark on a brand messaging course that will inspire you to write copy that consistently leads with authenticity and customer value by making every word count.

A truly memorable story can only be told once, which makes your job of crafting unique and personal brand narratives so incredibly important. No pressure ... but your clients, customers, and prospects are all counting on you.

Let's get started.

PART ONE

THE TRUTH ABOUT HEADLINES

A POWERFUL HEADLINE IGNITES THE CURIOSITY.

What separates short-lived brands from those that evolve and grow, and stay with us over the course of years or even decades?

Think about the brands you use every day—specifically, those with whom you actually enjoy engaging. You know the ones. They're really good at trailing you over the course of your often-unpredictable life, managing to keep up with your ever-changing interests. They stay close, but never intrude. They're there when you need them, but invisible when you want them to be. Even more impressive, though subtle, they maintain an authentic relevance that begs you to continue inviting them into your consumer world, over and over again.

That is what an authentic brand copywriter does. This is what you can do. And it all starts with a compelling headline.

Getting to the desired action

In news media, headlines sell. Period. In the world of marketing communications, they are also designed to sell—but offer an added pivotal component. They are designed to inspire interest and to set unique ideas in motion that support your brand's promise and encourage the reader to engage. And make no mistake, only the best headlines rise to the top and achieve the holy grail of page clicks and taps, getting the audience to actually read the content and drive them to the desired action: the like, the share, the download, the sale.

> Conversely, if the marketing asset lacks a compelling headline—whether it's a print or digital ad, landing page, datasheet, or nurture email campaign—everything that follows will be a wasted effort. You know it, and I know it. When it comes to brand messaging, the most critical challenge in sales and marketing is getting your audience past the headline.
>
> **The most critical challenge is getting your audience past the headline.**

The good news is that you can absolutely do it. You can write authentic headlines that will improve content engagement, positively influence your audience, and move the marketing needle toward increased sales and revenue.

But beware of the myth: There is no silver bullet for creating a viral headline. It all rests on you—your intimate knowledge of the audience and topic, your finely-honed messaging skills, your common sense, and a genuine desire to speak with your readership authentically.

I believe at the heart of every good headline is an emoting

component. It's an emotion, feeling, or sense you wish the reader to experience. This is good, as emotional headlines drive interactions that lead to increased readership. For example, let's take this fictitious headline:

"5 Harsh Truths about Copywriters"

Wow. Now there's a headline that's sure to get a copywriter's attention. Is it good news? Is it bad news? Do I (a copywriter) need to be concerned? I gotta know! This is an impactful headline. And why? If it were the headline of a real article or marketing asset, its success would rest on these key factors:

- The author knows his or her audience.
- It's short and to the point.
- It's curious and provocative.
- It's (presumably) in proper context (i.e., it lives in a publication written for copywriters).
- It creates a desire to gain knowledge.
- It potentially offers enlightenment or solves a problem.
- It uses numbers as a hook, an effective method for getting a reader's attention.

Most of all, it's authentic. Assuming the asset directly reveals the meaning of the headline, there's no hidden agenda. Just be aware that exploiting human curiosity can be sensitive territory, so proceed with caution. As long as your message isn't deceptive or manipulative, readers are generally open to entertaining their curious side.

Here's one more:

"10 Writing Tips That Will Make You Feel Like a Pro"

There is nothing more inviting than a headline that promises a positive experience. What writer doesn't want to feel like a pro, right? Notice the use of "make you feel." Though commonly used, I've found that this word choice ranks high among impactful headline phrases—especially when writing content for social media.

Here's why this headline works:

- Though longer, the number of words is ideal for the sentiment.
- It promises an emotional experience.
- The author knows his or her audience.
- It's in proper context.
- It invites the reader to learn more.
- It potentially solves a problem.
- And, once again, a number is used as a hook.

Other headline primers might include:

- Learn how …
- Don't miss …

- Top X tips for …
- X reasons why …
- The X best …
- Here's why …

You get the picture.

> **COPY TIP**
>
> While there may not be a hard and fast formula for the perfect headline, you'll begin to notice that they share common mission-critical characteristics:
>
> - Know your audience.
> - Keep word/character count short and to the point (or appropriate for the sentiment).
> - Introduce an emotion (e.g., curiosity, inspiration, joy, enlightenment).
> - Leave the reader wanting to learn more.
> - Solve a problem.
> - Use numbers as a hook when appropriate.
> - Promise an emotional experience.

Apart from these characteristics, there is another key element at play—one that's not so obvious. It's the way in which a reader actually perceives a headline.

While you may or may not realize it, as professional copywriters we are always striving to appeal to the consumer's subconscious mind—the part of their brain that is fundamentally curious and that wants to engage—whether they consciously realize it or not. A powerful headline ignites the curiosity. It speaks to our basic need to learn, understand, grow, and evolve.

If you acknowledge this, respect it, and mindfully integrate this sensitive understanding into your work, you will succeed famously as an authentic copywriter.

And, of course, what follows the headline should never disappoint. It should always live up to—if not exceed—the promise of the headline with quality, thoughtful, and relatable content.

Let's talk about body copy.

PART TWO

CONSTRUCTING BODY COPY

DON'T BE A MESSENGER TEASE.

Congratulations. You've mastered the elusive skill of creating an engaging headline—you've got the reader's attention. You've piqued their interest and delivered a cliff-hanging hook like no other. But don't pat yourself on the back just yet. The real work is just beginning.

So, now what?

Let's start with not being a messenger tease. Follow-through is now an obligation and a responsibility on your part. You've earned their precious, fleeting attention, and now you owe them a story.

There's nothing more frustrating than cashing in a click or a tap off a good headline, only to be exposed to body copy that's completely void of structure or purpose, or delivers a completely mistimed or misfired message. Worse yet is experiencing the harsh disappointment of being deceived by a headline that's only purpose was to get you "in," sans a well-crafted, relevant story to back it up.

I have no time or patience for that. And neither do your readers.

You know what I mean. You've lived it, too. What makes you think your readers are any different? I always reflect on these poor marketing asset experiences to sensitize myself before embarking on crafting a worthy and qualified storytelling experience for my readers. It's the golden rule, right? Treat others as you'd like to be treated. Give 'em something they want to read. Offer them a learning opportunity, something valuable, relatable, and useful that will enrich their personal or professional lives in some way.

Go ahead, make their day—if even for the brief time it takes them to read through your body copy.

Research. Then research some more.

Where do you begin the journey of body copy creation? Research. And then research some more.

If you've been writing for any length of time at all, this fact should come as no surprise to you. The foundation of good storytelling is knowing your subject matter through diligent research. Like the carpenter who measures twice and cuts once, our efforts as copywriters are wasted if not founded on the research necessary to convey our client's story the right way—the first time.

One of the things I enjoy most about being a copywriter is the opportunity it offers to learn a wealth of information about topics, products, and services I may otherwise know little or nothing about. If you're fortunate enough to be writer for a broad range of clients, it gets even more exciting to be exposed to a wide and interesting variety of industries and ideas—from retail and entertainment to finance and technology, and every imaginable topic in between. Never a dull moment, or a dull project.

Besides, who can argue the benefits of constantly learning new stuff? I've discovered that researching new topics makes my brain cells fire in consistently new ways, expanding my capacity and ability to learn. I believe it helps me adapt to change better and even increases the speed at which I can learn new things. Plus, (and here's a perk) it helps minimize boredom in my work. But most importantly, I think the greater the exposure we have to new and different topics and ideas—and the more experienced we get at writing about them—the more valuable we become to our clients.

If you've recently entered the field of marketing copywriting and thought your research-filled college days were over—surprise! They're just beginning. And if you're a seasoned copywriter, you are already living this reality and, hopefully, enjoying this very important process as you continue to evolve your skills in crafting authentic content.

A copywriter's role as mediator

As copywriters it's on us to play the part of a mediator, a pseudo–subject matter expert (SME); someone who precariously hangs in the balance between an actual SME and the content messaging task that lies ahead. To be clear, I never consider myself an SME; other than on the topic of my experience as a copywriter. Just because I'm writing about a certain topic doesn't mean I'm an expert on the subject—it just means I'm good (hopefully) at researching and gathering the information needed to build a story that resonates with the intended audience.

The good news is that, once you start digging, there's no

shortage of information to be found on virtually any existing topic. It's there. You just need to unearth it. Your fact-finding research should include interviews with SMEs, internet scouring, and source verification, to name a few. And once the data-gathering efforts are complete, the fun begins.

It's time to sort through, filter, and pan for the nuggets of gold that will help you tell the story.

The story arc

I won't dive too deep into the story arc, as it's likely a framework from which you are already operating—whether you consciously realize it or not. Newer copywriters treat it like a meditative mantra, while experienced ones do it instinctively with little or no conscious thought. It is the narrative arc, or story arc.

A story of any kind simply isn't a story without a beginning [framing the problem], a middle [describing the challenges or conflict], and an end [a resolution]. The story arc creates the foundation of the body copy that ultimately shapes the story. It's a sequence of events that takes the reader's imagination on a Tour de France of the topic at hand and sets the pace for, hopefully, a happy ending.

Readers of marketing content are no different. Good body copy is grounded in a basic story arc structure. Every time. Without it, like a moviegoer at a bad flick, the reader will simply give up and walk out—fast. The only thing that differentiates one story arc from another is the level of complexity (or simplicity) the content requires of it to stay on point.

As with any good story—whether it's a short, nurture campaign email or a long-form whitepaper—the story arc is vital for engaging your readers. Conversely, think about a time you watched a bad movie or read a disappointing book. It either fell short of properly setting up the plot or failed miserably at delivering a satisfactory conclusion—or the message in the middle was so confusing you simply gave up on it.

> **As with any good story, the story arc is vital for engaging your reader.**

Think of the classic three-act play:

Act 1: The scenario is set, and the reader is introduced to the problem or challenge.

Act 2: The reader is engaged in a narrative that exemplifies the problem to be solved, usually climaxing with a conflict.

Act 3: Miraculously, a resolution is introduced—a happy ending.

The role of subheads

Body copy, especially longer-form marketing assets like datasheets and whitepapers, should be a bit more forgiving to the reader. That is, unlike a digital ad or any ultrashort content piece, the longer-prose assets require more staying power on behalf of the reader. After all, there's a lot of content there—and a good chance they'll get winded along the way trying to power through it all (as interesting and engaging as it may be).

The solution? Subheads. Technically, they are secondary headlines that consistently support the main headline or premise. Functionally, they are welcomed "breathers" for the reader. More than just providing a break within multiple pages of content, they also help readers scan, pause, move ahead, or jump to any copy block with far more ease than without their aid.

Chances are, the first thing a potential reader is going to do is scan the paper to see what topics—or subheads—are covered within the document. So, make them count. They should be short and say precisely what the copy block addresses. For example, this chapter on constructing body copy contains subheads. This allows the reader (you) to jump around or quickly reference back to a section as desired.

Once again, there's no magic rule on their use. However, like commas and periods, I'd suggest using subheads when you feel there is a natural break in body copy flow or introduction to a new supporting idea.

Pull quotes

Like subheads, pull quotes are more commonly found in long-form marketing assets, providing a visual break in streams of copy. But their purpose is far more unique and strategic.

They serve primarily to entice readers into the full marketing asset, catering to those who prefer scanning first before diving in to read more. On multipage marketing assets, I generally use one pull quote per page—unless that page is already occupied by an image, figure, or infographic. Strategically

> A pull quote is an excerpt taken directly from the body copy, then placed in proximity of the copy source to emphasize the importance or relevance of the topic. To help them draw even greater attention, they're usually emphasized by larger font so they stand out more prominently. Whenever appropriate, I prefer using brand colors for the pull quote text rather than plain black for highlighting their presence.
>
> **Pull quotes entice readers into the full marketing asset.**

placed pull quotes can be effective; however, too many on a single page can distract the reader—and possibly discourage them from reading the full content.

Get personal with your narrative

Nothing resonates stronger than a marketing asset that personally calls out to the reader. In effect, the copy says, "Hey, you. Yeah, you. I'm talking to you." Shifting your tone from a third-party informative perspective to a second-person storytelling approach can reap big returns.

Whenever possible and appropriate, make the narrative personal. It's one thing to drone on endlessly about features and benefits (F&Bs)—things that are, admittedly, critical to call out. But the effectiveness of your brand storytelling will fall short if you don't directly tie those beloved F&Bs to a real-world experience that your reader can vividly imagine and personally relate to. This is accomplished, in part, by communicating your story in a one-to-one personal dialogue.

In other words, make it real and personal for your reader.

Don't fall into the trap of treating a brand like a "thing;" some ominous, inanimate object that requires delicate handling. Humanize it. Make it real. This is the only way you can connect authentically with your audience. After all, if what you're writing about provides a real value or solves a real-world challenge for the reader, shouldn't your message reflect that? It's the difference between what I think of as feature-centric and value-centric messaging.

Let's take this fictitious men's razor pitch as an example:

Feature-centric
"[Product X] delivers a close shave, thanks to its stainless steel, four-blade cartridge and sturdy handle construction."

Versus

Value-centric
"A man armed with [Product X] understands the *real* benefits of a close shave. Just ask his girlfriend."

Bam. Mic drop. You get the picture. Yeah, it's great that the razor has all those gadgety cool features. But in the end, well … sometimes it's just more important to place emphasis on the user experience.

> **COPY TIP**
>
> Have some fun with it. Good storytelling helps humanize your brand, product, or service. And it works for both short- and long-form marketing assets. The art of copywriting is one of the best ways to connect and build relationships—and the more authentic and consistent the "voice" you use, the better. Remember to keep it real with body copy that won't disappoint.

Next up: the call to action.

PART THREE

THE CALL TO ACTION

USE CTAs LIBERALLY TO BOOST CONVERSIONS.

The journey from prospect to customer can be complicated, which makes your job as a copywriter ever so strategic. There's a lot riding on the words you choose to engage your readers. Say the wrong thing to the wrong audience at the wrong time—or any combination of these copywriting fails—and you've lost them. And good luck trying to get them back. But do it right, and you and the reader are on your way to a wonderfully symbiotic relationship; the reader enters the sales funnel and/or gets the cool thing you've so eloquently described, and you get to keep your job. See how that works?

Now that you've created some amazing body copy packed with customer value and authentic sentiment, your reader wants more. Do you leave them hanging to build suspense and provoke anticipation for the next act? Tempting, but no. Cliffhangers may work in a classic '80s television drama series, but there's no place for them in a marketing asset.

Especially when the reader is engaged and ready—now—to take the relationship to the next level.

Enter the call to action, or CTA, the critical messaging component that can bridge the gap between a lead and a conversion, a prospect and a customer, or an acquaintance and a long-term relationship. Get the reader to click, tap, or act on a CTA, and you're on your way.

Don't be coy
Now's not the time to be shy. You've invested a lot of time and careful consideration crafting a message that has successfully connected with your reader—that's a good thing. But now they're expecting even more. They want to know what they need to do now to buy, download, subscribe, or sign up for your offer.

Here's something I learned early on: readers actually look for the "Buy Now!" or other CTA and feel confused or even frustrated when they don't find it in the marketing asset. You've already told them what they'll get. Now tell them how to get it. You owe them that. But for gosh sake, don't make them read your mind (we all know how that works out in relationships). Go for the close—and make it easy, intuitive, and obvious about what to do next.

CTAs: Here, there, everywhere
As copywriters, we pride ourselves on weaving clever phrases and snappy quips into our content. We strive to deliver just the right balance of enticing information and product knowledge, then sprinkle it with a bit of mystique to keep the reader engaged. This generally works in most messaging formats. But not the CTA.

> The key to a successful CTA is predictability. That's right. Put away the James Bond self-exploding, intelligence-gathering pen, and pick up the number-two pencil—predictability rules in the world of CTAs. Readers already know what they want and those magic words that will deliver it. So, go ahead, use CTAs generously and make them obvious—and short.
>
> **Predictability rules in the world of CTAs.**

Here are some classic go-to CTAs that just keep on giving:

- Buy Now
- Register Here
- Order Now
- Call Today
- Download Now
- Subscribe Here
- Pay Now
- Sign Up

May I have another?

With CTAs, it pays to be predictable—and generous. If they're so great—and so effective—is it okay to have more than one CTA in a given marketing asset? Absolutely, if the content messaging supports it and they don't conflict.

I used to buy into the rumor that there should only be a single CTA on a page or asset, but not anymore. Having multiple CTAs can work, but to be clear, we're addressing the value of having multiple placements of the same or related CTA, which offers the reader more chances to convert or act at any point within the marketing asset.

Conversely, be sure to avoid multiple unique or conflicting CTAs; that is, they should always directly complement each other. Taking the reader in multiple directions will cause confusion and can result in inertia—compromising the purpose of the CTA. Worse yet, the reader will likely give up and make no choice at all. Not good.

Caveats aside, use CTAs liberally and strategically to boost conversions. Readers will appreciate having ample opportunities to act in their favor. And there are hundreds of ways to use them—basically, any time you want the reader to do something or respond in some way, whether to sign up, download a PDF, fill out a form, or buy a product. The actions are limitless. The fact is, they can go just about anywhere. And they should. Just be sure they are relevant and easy to spot.

The CTA is a staple on any print or online marketing asset and can live just about anywhere—from banner ads, email campaigns, and landing pages to datasheets, whitepapers, and customer stories. Don't ever underestimate the value of the CTA; it's the key that unlocks the offer with just one simple click, tap, or phone call.

COPY TIP

Be sure you understand the difference between a CTA and reference links. The latter can actually distract the reader and undermine your messaging goals. This can be tricky. While links within body copy can sometimes work if you're connecting them to a related source—like a landing page to register for an event you're promoting—you should minimize opportunities for readers to click away from your marketing asset, as you stand the chance of not getting them back.

PART FOUR

COPYEDITING

MESSAGING REFINEMENT FOR HIGH-PERFORMANCE MARKETING COPY.

Copywriters help their clients formulate ideas about their product and brand, which includes frank (and often lengthy) discussions about the strategic use and intention of the marketing asset as well as conversion expectations. All of this, together, influences how the copy will be written—its length, voice, tone, and medium.

Copyediting, on the other hand, is the task (and a process I enjoy most) of messaging refinement. It involves ensuring that the content is factual, technically correct (from the standpoint of features and benefits), and most of all, flows well. When we put our copyeditor hats on, we pivot from fact-finding to story refinement, shifting into proofreading mode for grammar correction and sentence structure alignment. This can mean adding content—or eliminating redundancies—for optimal clarity.

Some corporate creative teams and agencies alike prefer

to keep the two disciplines distinctly apart. And with good reason, mainly because, as a general rule, it's not a good idea for a writer to edit his or her own content (we've all heard that before). This division of labor allows the copywriter to focus their time on research and the arduous task of transforming their findings into a storyline. Copyeditors are then freed up to primarily focus on the critical task of messaging refinement.

But if you're like me, oftentimes you're tasked with both roles. Not ideal, but also not impossible to manage. Here's a process I follow that helps me be effective in both roles:

The 80 percent push

Taking on a new writing assignment—especially longer-form marketing assets—can seem overwhelming, even for the seasoned copywriter. And with deadlines always looming, the process seems to demand the need for clear benchmarks to ease the task at hand and optimize creative output.

I begin every writing endeavor with the end in mind of initially constructing an 80 percent draft, or as I like to call it, the 80 percent push. The 80 percent push represents what I consider to be the heavy lifting of document creation—the initial liftoff phase that includes the tedious research, SME wrangling and interviewing, fact-gathering, and time-consuming process of tying it all together into a workable storyline.

The 80 percent push represents the heavy lifting of document creation.

Maybe it's just a mind game I play on my myself, but culling out this stage as almost a separate project within a project works for me. If your process doesn't already include this phase or something similar, give it a try.

It's a process (more of a mind-set) that I've used throughout my career, and it has never let me down. Basically, this mind-set allows me to mentally break down the writing assignment into more manageable milestones and relieves my mind of grappling with the image of completing the entire project—from notes to outline to draft to publication ready—in one (often overwhelming) step. It's a key milestone that separates the initial drafting phase from the refinement stage.

I know myself. And for me the initial drafting stage can be the most intense in terms of grunt work. Let's not kid ourselves, it's probably like this for most copywriters. After all, we have to be instant pseudo experts on virtually any given topic—and usually on a moment's notice. Not an easy feat, but nonetheless a skill that requires constant practice if we're to stay sharp in our field.

Shelf it

Once I've achieved the 80 percent draft, I've earned a break—for both mental and strategic reasons.

To my point earlier, I'm often tasked with both copywriting and copyediting. You might be too. Not always ideal, but a professional reality just the same. So, shelfing a project at the 80 percent draft stage is critical, serving two key purposes. One, I find that it allows me to breathe and mentally break away from the arduous task of pulling the storyline together. After all, that was a lot of work, so this is a step I very much look forward to and greet enthusiastically with a sigh of relief and a mental high five.

Secondly, it provides a critical opportunity to separate myself from the content as long as the deadline will tolerate it. We know that editing our own content immediately after drafting won't serve us well, as whatever errors or oversights we may have originally included during the drafting process (albeit unintentionally) will still be there—and we still won't see them.

Once you complete the initial draft, shelf it for as long as you can—the longer amount of time between drafting and editing, the better. This critical break frees up the mind and reenergizes our creative juices, preparing us to take on the copyediting phase with fresh eyes and a refreshed perspective so we can deliver optimal editing results.

Negotiating copyedits

The art of feedback. Or as I like to call it, negotiating copyedits. We may consider ourselves as skilled copywriters who are experienced in crafting engaging content, eloquently and with proper grammar (with the aid, of course, of a handy style guide). And most of the time our clients see us that way, too.

Most of the time.

Sometimes though—no matter how much effort, time, and passion you put into a marketing asset—the client sees it differently. And that's okay. After all, we don't know everything, and if we remain open-minded to constructive, honest feedback we'll gain a new perspective on the topic that may also allow us to grow professionally.

To be frank, most of us don't always enjoy the feedback process. It can get messy. After all, it exposes us to criticism and vulnerability—not to mention, once an opinion is asked for, there's no telling what we'll get in return from the SME and other stakeholders. But that's okay. It's all part of the creative process—the delicate, necessary dance between SME and copywriter that eventually gets everyone to the desired end result.

But what do you do when you get feedback that, quite frankly, is wrong or inappropriate? It's happened to me, and I'm willing to bet it's happened to you too. My first go-to strategy is to simply respond to the feedback with objective counter feedback—whether it be a style issue, a lesson on correct grammar usage, or proper sentence structure. The responsibility is on us to provide a clear, objective, and politely stated explanation that supports our professional opinion on the matter. This usually works. Clients are generally grateful to know we have their best interests in mind and only want to ensure that their marketing efforts are successful. But even if there's pushback, it's important to negotiate—tactfully—to arrive, at the very least, at a happy medium to achieve content that flows properly (and is grammatically correct), while retaining the integrity of the SME's voice. This is always the goal.

At other times, however, SMEs simply want content to be written their way, even if it is (dare I say) grammatically incorrect or doesn't present the topic in its best light. Pick your reason. These are the times I've learned to just let it go. Like you, I take great pride in my work and believe that everything I produce should be portfolio worthy. But that's not always the case. I've humbly accepted that there are some things in the development of marketing copy that are simply not right, but must be tolerated. Not ideal, but a reality.

Like any relationship, good negotiating skills are key. Always be empathetic, objective, and professional while negotiating what you believe is in the best interest of your client. But in the end, it's their project—not yours.

Don't fight it. Every now and then you need to take one for the team.

Know your style guide

Most copywriters have at least one (if not several) style guides on hand. They are prepared, knowing that the preference of style guides can vary among clients for a variety of reasons, so it's important they're familiar with the ones most commonly used for crafting marketing content.

Style guides for business and marketing, such as the *Associated Press Style Book* (AP), *Chicago Manual of Style*, and *APA Style*, offer a set of generally accepted standards for the writing and design of documents—in this case, marketing content for the general reading audience. They cover everything from simple things like grammar and punctuation to more substantive questions about citation, layout, or format. Some guides also address writing styles as they apply to content and voice.

For most organizations, following a style guide consistently is critical, especially when writing content that supports brand messaging across all mediums. The style guide helps ensure uniformity in style and formatting across all content types, helping copywriters retain the brand's authenticity in voice, tone, and style.

If you're a copywriter for corporate marcom, pick one and stick with it. If you freelance or work with an agency, be sure to ask your client which style they prefer. And if they don't know, offer to recommend one. They'll be grateful you're thinking about their best interests.

Keep your SEO in check

Search Engine Optimization (SEO) copywriting is a specialized style of content writing that purposefully contains key words and phrases that your target audience will likely use to search specific information on the web. As copywriters, we search the internet almost daily as part of the fact-finding process of content development. For example, if we want to learn about copywriting or specifically brand copywriting, we type those words in the search bar to see what pops up. Based on the feedback we get, we narrow down our search by being even more specific.

This works because SEO copywriters fortify online content with strategic key words and phrases. The more targeted and specific the key words used, the higher the online content will rank in search results—and the faster our targeted audience will get the content types they're looking for.

SEO copywriting helps drive qualified traffic. And it's our job to make sure that happens.

SEO copywriters are generally highly specialized in the digital content space and work closely with copyeditors to ensure that final drafts are complemented with optimized SEO content before they go live online. In addition to SEO copywriters, key words and phrases may also be provided by an SEO strategist or, oftentimes, directly from the client. But if neither is the case, and this is yet another hat you need to wear in addition to copywriter and copyeditor, don't dismay. You can do this.

Part of our job as copywriters means we're already trained to understand people—to have a sense of what appeals to them and what doesn't, in the context of crafting marketing assets. Call it empathy, intuition, or whatever, we go deep to better understand—authentically—what our readers want. From there, we strategically choose just the right words and phrases that appeal, delight, and persuade—encouraging them to take a desired action. This knowledge and skill set can also serve you well when it's time to craft SEO keywords and phrases.

Along with the process of document creation for any project, you should always be considering the importance of tailoring content for online searches—fortifying headlines, subheads, and body copy with recommended key words and phrases. Decide upfront which key words you'll want to focus on, or if you have access to an SEO specialist, consult with that person for guidance. Either way, know in advance what those search terms are for the topic before you put pen to paper.

Those terms that will be central to your overall message will likely be the same ones readers will use to search out your content. It's important that the words and phrases you use are common enough that most people would use them but specific enough to your marketing asset that you optimize the chance of getting a high search ranking on it.

For example, "copywriting" vs. "marketing copywriting" vs. "brand copywriting."

Why is SEO copywriting important? Think of SEO

keyword phrases as first cousins to the headline, only rather than having them strictly adorned across the top of the marketing asset, they're sprinkled throughout the content that serve to improve online search rankings and help drive traffic to your online publication.

Every word counts in SEO. And depending on the type and length of the publication, the number of key words can vary. Personally, I've found that a minimum of three to five terms work ideally, but I understand that up to fifteen is fine if the content type and topic warrants that amount. Find out what has worked best for your clients and adjust as needed.

One last but important consideration is ensuring that, once you've selected the recommended search words and phrases, you integrate them organically into the asset. In other words, don't force key words into the copy if they don't naturally flow with the brand narrative. Oftentimes some recommended key words simply won't align with the brand vocabulary, so simply choose the ones that work organically and ignore the ones that don't.

Selecting and placing the right SEO words can help optimize the attention and number of readers where you want them. Pick the wrong ones, and well, the full potential of the marketing asset may never be realized. So, choose well and choose wisely. Your hard work—and the conversion goals of your client—are riding on it.

A welcome ally

A good copyeditor is a natural. Sure, it takes time and experience to hone professional editing skills, but those with a natural-born instinct have their talent "turned on" all the time—even outside work. Are you that person that notices every grammar fail and oversight in everything and everywhere you go? If so, embrace it. You're a naturally talented messaging refinement guru and are an ideal candidate with whom to form a close ally for creating high-performing marketing copy.

While to non–marketing professionals it may seem minor, copyediting is a critical step in the copy development process and can have a huge impact on engagement and conversion. It's an artform that more than refines the marketing message, it can help refine the brand—and your customer's trust in it—making the difference between a curious prospect and customer for life.

PART FIVE

EMAIL SUBJECT LINES

GETTING READERS EXCITED AT THE PROSPECT OF WHAT'S INSIDE.

A word on email subject lines.

In many ways, email subject lines function very much like headlines. They are the first component of your email communication that has a shot at engaging your targeted audience, acting as a preemptive hook to get your reader to open, read, and act on the offer.

Not an easy task.

Think of your email audience as a popular club, with each of your subscribers having their own private bouncer. That means unless you're part of the "in crowd," your chances of getting in are slim—at least right away. Therein lies the challenge and the mission: to get past the bouncer (i.e., your prospect's finite attention) via an engaging subject line that's relevant, authentic, and timely.

Crafting email subject lines requires strategy and a

finely-honed knowledge of the targeted audience, as well as an instinct for just the right message to entice them.

What makes a good email subject line?

The most effective email subject lines are those that are both compelling and informative, but don't give away too much (readers will anticipate getting more from the headline and body copy once opened). No matter what clever combination of creativity you whip up, in the end it needs to pique interest or provoke curiosity. If the subject line isn't compelling for your subscribers, game over. And there goes the inside links to your product promotion or to that thought leadership blog you worked so hard on.

As a copywriting wizard, your goal is to boost email open rates. Period.

Nurture email campaigns can center on a wide variety of offerings including sales, products and services, event registrations, webinar invites, marketing asset downloads, white papers, or blog promotions. Here are just a few classic examples of proven subject line approaches that can help increase open rates:

- **Learning opportunities**: "How to Boost Email Open Rates in One Easy Lesson"

- **Self-improvement**: "Learn How to Decrease Your Writing Time and Get Better Results"

- **Leading with numbers**: "5 Sure-Fire Writing Strategies for Boosting Open Rates"

- **Solution Oriented**: "Minimize Editing Rounds and Maximize Profits"

- **Exclusivity**: "The Only Book You'll Ever Need to Write High-Performance Copy"

- **Expertise**: "Learn First Hand from Top Experts on Winning Copywriting Strategies"

- **Fear of Missing Out**: "Don't Miss This One-Time Webinar on Email Campaign Strategy"

- **Curiosity**: "You Won't Believe This One Common Trait All Copywriters Share"

- **Reference**: "10 Tips for Writing Authentic Marketing Copy"

Testing, testing …

The combination of approaches to crafting a winning email subject line is almost endless. There is also an equally endless number of ways to approach the same email differently, so whenever feasible be sure to A/B test; that is, compare two or more messaging approaches to determine which performs better. Even if you have a proven, high-performing email, don't be afraid to put it to the test over time.

In short, a successful email subject line not only convinces readers to open your email, but it gets them excited at the prospect of what's inside for them—a new product solution, insight, or learning opportunity. Whatever you hope for them to gain all hinges on your time, talent, and choice of words to get past the email bouncer.

PART SIX

BLOGGING

BLOGGING IS AN OPPORTUNITY TO HUMANIZE THE BRAND.

As emphasized earlier under the section on constructing body copy, take every opportunity to get personal with your brand narrative. And no other online marketing medium lends itself more ideally for exploiting the personal side of your brand than blogging.

 I'm a big fan of blogs—both as an avid reader of them and of their use as a key component to an overall brand-building strategy. As a copywriter, one of the things I enjoy most about blogging is the opportunity it provides to humanize the brand. It's a fantastic way to connect authentically with your readership, providing a unique platform for expressing the things you're truly passionate about—while staking the ground of thought leadership in your industry.

Build industry thought leadership and your brand
Done well, blog posts can both simultaneously build consumer trust and raise your brand's likability. A powerful way to communicate with your prospects and customers, a well-thought-out blogging strategy can build your brand with a loyal following and directly result in conversions. Why? Because loyal readers are loyal for reason. They have learned to trust in the content that you share and even begin to rely on it to help them make relevant purchase and lifestyle decisions.

This is the payoff for blogging done right.

And, yes, while blogs are often entertaining and fun to read (and, in my opinion, they should be), their true value triumphs when they're grounded in thought leadership—offering unique insights, knowledge, and learning opportunities that build trust and, ultimately, influence the readership.

One of the most singularly desired goals of every brand is to stand out—to establish itself and the organization as an expert in the industry. This shared knowledge and expertise through online blogging gradually builds you up as an authority in your field so that your brand is top-of-mind when your readership is ready to purchase.

As for word count, don't get too hung up on that. I've found that, on average, a B2B blog can fall anywhere between five hundred and eight hundred words; but, in my experience, the quality of the content rules here, not the quantity. Word count should directly relate to how many words are actually needed to tell your story. As long as the content is engaging, relevant, and considerate of their time overall, readers won't mind hanging in there until the end—long or short.

COPY TIP

Here are some of the characteristics I believe make blogs appealing and bring me back for more:

- They make a singular point (i.e., they avoid conflicting or competing content).
- They stay on point (i.e., no pontificating).
- They are personal and conversational in nature (i.e., they are talking to me).
- They lack ranting or competition bashing.
- They interject a sense of humor or the lighter side of the topic.
- They are credible, believable, and, when appropriate, backed by legitimate sources.

Be consistent about keeping your blog topics on mark with what your audience wants to read. Timing and relevance, like all brand copywriting, is everything.

PART SEVEN

WRITING FOR THE WEB

ELEVATE YOUR BRAND VOICE IN A MORE PERSONAL, INFORMAL STYLE OF WRITING.

Ah, the 1990s. Among other timeless notables, they brought us the ever-popular *Friends* TV show, Beanie Babies, and of course, the World Wide Web—or, as more affectionately known today, the internet.

Almost overnight, the internet completely transformed the way consumers learn, buy, sell, and socialize. Like a dusty old basement lamp that suddenly got turned on, the internet shed a whole new light on not only how we consume branded content but also how marketers create it. This nascent phenomenon—which would become foundational to every marketing communications and brand strategy—went even further, creating a whole new marketing medium and inspiring copywriters to develop content in a style unique for the online world.

Today, it's become commonplace for marketing content developers to toggle between print and web. In some larger agencies and corporate marketing communications settings, specialty writers are often assigned to each medium, as each requires a unique writing style of its own. Either way, both styles critically depend on one very important aspect: that the copywriter knows the brand story and knows it well.

In fact, you (the copywriter) should know it so well that you can tell it a dozen different ways—without ever diluting the brand's essence. From the elevator pitch to long-form white papers and the web, your job is to know your brand story so well you can adapt it to suit any medium.

The dynamism of web content

When people pick up a book or magazine—or most printed marketing assets—they do so with an intention of reading it. They wish to learn something new, engage in self-development, or simply lose themselves in a story for pure entertainment. It is purposeful engagement.

But unlike the experience with printed publications, most web readers generally don't read web content word-for-word. As I've learned over the years, it's generally the opposite. Webpage visitors are typically in search mode—they're on an internet mission, scanning quickly from page to page, section to section, looking only for headlines, subheads, or callouts that satisfy their specific search criteria.

Webpage visitors are typically in search mode—they're on an internet mission.

What's really different between print and web? When I'm tasked with crafting web copy, I regularly engage with knowledgeable web and digital experts to help me refine my messaging so it's worthy of web publication—and I encourage you to do the same. Here are a few fundamentals I've picked up along the way that help me better understand what makes web content stand apart from print: length, tone, and SEO.

Length

Because of limited attention spans—and the fact that consumers tend to avoid prolonged reading on computer screens (let's face it, the glare can get annoying)—web content is intentionally crafted in smaller, more easily consumable copy blocks. When a visitor does land on a website, be cognizant that you've got precious little time to capture their attention with a clear, concise, and engaging story. They've surfed the Net looking for something specific—and presumably found it on your web page. So, don't let them down. Keep it short, relevant, compelling, and above all, authentic.

Tone

This differentiator is my personal favorite. The nature of web content allows the brand copywriter to break away from the often mundane tonality (and style guides) of other marketing mediums and elevate their voice in a far more personal, informal style of writing. If there was ever a marketing medium for copywriters to exude their true personality, web is the place. Web readers want personal dialogue—and expect it. Unlike writing for a general audience, web content—particularly blogs and other online publications—are crafted for a specific audience. Think of it as having a one-on-one conversation, which is why, done right, web content is such a powerful marketing tool in today's digital world. Nothing elevates the impact of web content like convincing the reader you're speaking directly to them.

SEO

Albeit tactical, SEO is uniquely important to creating web content. This means tackling your story or brand message from both the front and back end. On the front end, you want to be sure and fortify your web content with strategic, carefully chosen key words and phrases that directly impact the success of would-be audiences finding and landing on your content. It's all about helping them narrow down their search so they can find you—and your content—quicker. The more specific, the better, and the higher online content will rank in search results. And, of course, once you've successfully got them there, it's your job to be sure your content steps up to the test on the back end—it needs to deliver, not disappoint (see everything previously mentioned in this book).

Internet matchmaking

In some fundamental ways, web content isn't much different from print—at least in spirit. Though the technical approach is uniquely different, web messaging should be crafted to shape the brand story and the consumer's journey. And the end in mind is always the same: to tell a compelling story that matches the value of the brand with the right customers.

PART EIGHT

CUSTOMER PERSONAS

THE SUCCESS OF YOUR BRAND MESSAGING RESTS ON HOW WELL YOU KNOW YOUR TARGET AUDIENCE.

Human relationships are important. Not just because we want them but because we are social by nature and therefore hardwired to crave interactions. We need them. It's this unique power of human connection that satisfies our innate need to feel a sense of belonging, to feel part of something bigger—a tribe, a common cause, a greater purpose. But more than that, I believe, we're drawn to relationships because we want to feel understood and that we're not alone in our ongoing search to satisfy our basic needs and our desire to solve daily struggles so that we can grow and evolve—whatever that means for each of us.

We all have goals: personal, family, financial, business … the list goes on. So, we naturally seek out those with common desires in the hope and expectation to share our goals, understand them better through storytelling, learn more about ourselves in the process, and ultimately achieve our goals.

Let's face it. Without relationships, well, we'd be lonely. And so would your brand.

Brands don't survive on their own like lone-wolf renegades in old western movies. They are completely dependent upon relationships, specifically the ones you carefully curate and nurture over time through good will, trust, empathy, respect, and authenticity in approach and tone with your customers and prospects. We accomplish this by understanding our broader target audience or audiences—then take it a step further by creating buyer personas, also known as user, customer, prospect, consumer, or business personas.

What is a persona?

Dynamic, well-thought-out personas can have a defining impact on your marketing strategy. Why? Because by taking the time to develop them, you've significantly elevated the effectiveness of your brand messaging by making it personal. Among the generality often referred to as your target audience, creating personas means you've singled out individual customers and prospects within that target audience—semi-fictional characters that personify your ideal buyer—so you can personalize and cater your messaging to their unique buyer journey.

You may be surprised to learn that your target audience isn't always summed up in a singular persona. Many times, it's several. Your job is to parse them out from the generalities of your target audience and home in on specific buyer characteristics.

Buyer personas reveal the interests of your demographic, opening up a pivotal, strategic gateway to knowing who they are, their pain points, the resources they trust, and what's uniquely important to them. Creating user personas that represent your overall target audience can be fundamental to your marketing strategy, driving the direction of your content on a significantly more personal level, which can lead to more meaningful customer interactions and authentic relationships.

Personas drive the direction of your content on a significantly more personal level.

The success of your brand copywriting rests on how well you know your target audience.

What you need to know about your persona

In a nutshell, your job is to dig—and dig deep—to identify and understand what is fundamentally top of mind for your target audience. Like any relationship, it takes time, trust, and an ongoing conversation to truly understand personal nuances and their underlying motivators. Here's how you can begin to reveal your ideal buyer persona(s).

Start with the basics:

- How old are they—or what is their average age bracket?

- What is their relationship status and family dynamic?
- Where do they live?
- What are their general interests? Hobbies?
- What are their values?
- What social media platforms do they use?
- What's their income?

Then, dig a little deeper:

- What's their job title?
- What are their professional responsibilities?
- What keeps them up at night?
- What challenges do they face?
- What are their goals?
- What's important to them, and why?
- What are their budget constraints/considerations?

Where to get the data

In today's data-driven marketing world, information about your customers and prospects is—or should be—plentiful. Beyond your own understanding of who you think they might be, it's important to predicate that understanding on facts, and that means knowing where to look for—and how to get your strategic arms around—the insights that customer and prospect data can reveal. From these crucial insights you can begin to construct uniquely crafted buyer personas that will launch your efforts to create next-level, impactful brand messaging to greater heights.

So, where do you look? Here are some common resources for learning most of what, if not everything, you want to know about your ideal buyer persona:

- Interview the client or marketing manager.

- Survey current customers and prospects.

- Dive into web analytics—identify unique website page hits, where they visit most frequently, and for how long, as well as what's paid attention to and what's largely ignored.

- Consider results of current and past marketing campaigns. What does their success (or lack thereof) reveal about your audience?

- Review case studies and use cases.

Most importantly, check out your customer relationship management (CRM) tool. Today's CRMs come gratefully equipped with smart reporting tools from which you can draw rich insights from prospecting and sales activities. Look for key trends and identify common as well as unique needs across the customer and prospect spectrum, then evaluate those insights for commonalities. The more you look around within your own marketing arsenal, the more ways you'll discover the critical insights you need to know about who follows, trusts, and relies on your brand—and why.

Now that you've done the research, it's time to take all that big-picture data and begin to make it personal by creating a unique buyer persona—that special fictitious someone who is representative of your key audience.

Sample B2B Persona

There are many different ways to approach the structure of a buyer persona, particularly as you consider B2B vs B2C and the type of product, service, or offering your brand represents. No matter what the scenario or format you choose, make them personal. Use the first person, as if the persona is speaking directly to you—the brand copywriter—and telling you exactly what you need to know in order to appeal to their needs.

As an example, let's take a look at this B2B buyer persona and what it might look like for a developer of mobile computing devices:

Persona Name: Perl

Title: Developer, Mobile Computing

What does she do?
I design and develop the most powerful mobile computing devices for some of the largest global and domestic brands in the mobile computing industry.

What does she need?
I need cutting-edge technologies that deliver powerful, user-friendly processing capability that handles on-device machine learning.

What is her end in mind?
I want the ability to deliver an end-user experience

that's intelligent, intuitive, and powerful—and allows users to access data and information from wherever they are reliably and efficiently.

About me

I've been a developer for over five years. It's challenging, particularly because technology is always changing, making it increasingly difficult to stay competitive with other mobile computing device manufacturers. My success is predicated on the ability to quickly and easily stay abreast of the latest technology advances—then assess and integrate them in each product release. This agility also plays a key role in elevating my professional worth in the industry as a highly valued, sought-after developer.

Value for Perl

It's important for me to always be in the know of the latest technology advances, then leverage them in a way that expands—not limits—my imagination for creating a greater, more intuitive user experience. It's exciting for me to design and deliver devices that are rich with features and functionality that my customers really want.

Messages for Perl

- Deliver timely, relevant messaging on the latest mobile computing technologies.
- Illustrate uniqueness in features and functionality.
- Demonstrate quickly and clearly how product specs translate to improved UX.

- Eliminate barriers to crucial information on the latest technology solutions.

- Simplify access to learning opportunities on new solutions.

- Explain specific as well as broader implications of the technology's impact on her immediate projects and her career.

Stay current with buyer personas. Like relationships, personas change and evolve over time based on market trends, economic influencers, and technology advances to name a few. These evolving personas should always align with brand messaging strategy. Knowing who they are at every stage of their customer life cycle—right from the beginning—is critical to your success as a brand copywriter. For new and existing customers, you need to gain a thorough understanding of their brand perception, especially as it evolves over time, based on concrete evidence from your persona research.

Your customer persona as a good friend

There's only one way to reach your intended audience, and that's to know them and know them well. Keeping your customer persona or personas in mind allows you to create brand messaging content that's uniquely designed for a specific person, letting you present offerings in a timely and relatable manner.

Even though you're creating fictional customer personas as part of a larger marketing strategy, treat each one with a sense of realism and authenticity as though you're speaking to a good friend. In a sense, they are real, as they are representative of the very real people your product or service hopes to serve in some meaningful way.

Keep your personas simple, straightforward, up to date, and above all, personal.

PART NINE

WRITING FOR SOCIAL MEDIA

SOCIAL MEDIA CONTENT EXPONENTIALLY EXPANDS A BRAND'S REACH.

Social media taps into our primal need to socialize, interact, and connect with others in our human tribe. Socializing is fundamental for helping us maintain a healthy, balanced quality of life by helping each of us feel uniquely connected and empowered by shared experience. So, it's no surprise that social media platforms are so astoundingly popular for connecting, sharing, and learning with others around the globe. They provide a digitally connected window to more information—and more personal connections—than anyone could have ever imagined just a short couple of decades ago.

With a simple tap or click, anyone with a smart phone, mobile device, or computer can make friends or connect with like-minded people within and beyond international borders and around the globe. In a virtual instant, anyone can access the latest news, share common interests, make a new friend, seek career opportunities, discover new products—you name it—all at their fingertips and at minimum or no cost.

Social media exponentially extends the ability to instantly increase human connections, making it a crucial medium to leverage as part of an overall marketing and branding strategy.

So, what about copywriting for social media? How hard can it be? Certainly not as challenging as crafting white papers, product sheets, web content, or other longer-form marketing assets. Right? Not so fast. Don't underestimate the art and unique skill required to craft engaging microcontent for one of the most powerful, modern marketing mediums of today.

The swiping struggle is real

We all do it. As mesmerized by our mobile smart devices as we are, we probably spend more time swiping through dozens of screens of random posts, ads, .gifs, and other digital content than actually stopping to read, tap, comment, or share. And that's no surprise. Literally billions of content posts are populated across dozens of social media platforms every day. We simply don't have the attention span or mental capacity to capture or comprehend them all.

The Challenge: In today's digital world, brand copywriters face tech-savvy consumers who've mastered the single-finger skill of multidirectional swiping at near light speeds on their mobile smart devices. The digital attention market has become saturated, and consumer attention spans are at a premium.

The Mission: To create brand messaging that's attention-grabbing, compelling, and engaging for social media platforms, all the while combatting the challenges of limited word counts and even more limited digital attention spans.

So how do you grab the attention of your specific persona or target audience within the complex matrix of social media conversations? Challenging, but not impossible. Some of today's biggest and best of brands make social media content development a top priority because they see the value of—and return on—breaking through the digital clutter to attract and retain followers, which in turn feeds sales funnels and increases revenues.

Social media is an unsurpassed tool for distributing content, fast.

Great content doesn't share itself

Every successful marketing and branding campaign needs a channel for distribution, and there's no better modern method than social media. Hands down, it's an unsurpassed tool for distributing content—and fast. Let's face it, even the best of content doesn't distribute itself. Social media provides a super user-friendly platform for people to quickly and easily pass along content so the conversations you start can keep going and going.

Make no mistake, when your favorite pen (as it were) dips its proverbial ink in social media waters, you'll have your work cut out for you. Among some of the challenges unique to this modern online medium, you'll be combatting against an onslaught of attention jockeys—and they're all after the same precious sliver of attention from your digitally surfing audience. Your job is to stay laser focused on crafting precision, targeted social media messages to your ideal persona while staying true to the brand narrative.

Social media marketing enhances visibility, promotes growth, drives sales, and extends a brand's reach in ways no other marketing medium can. It opens doors that allow brand copywriters to have personal, one-on-one conversations with their ideal personas on one of the most powerful distribution channels. It doesn't get much better than that.

Messaging tips for the social media–minded

Writing for social media can be a little tricky, but once you get the hang of it, you'll discover just how engaging it can be—for both you and your audiences. Here's a few writing tips to ensure your voice, tone, and approach to crafting compelling, relevant content aligns with the social media vibe.

- **Know your brand voice.** Just because it's personal and informal doesn't give you permission to go off the brand narrative. What are your brand's values, and how are you going to get them across on social media? It should suit the reader, as well as the social media platform—without compromising your brand's value.

- **Make it personal.** Social media is a communication platform that very much thrives on personal, one-to-one, second-person interactions. Write like you're standing right in front of your ideal customer or prospect.

- **Watch your tone:** Remember, social media content is intrinsically powered by personal, one-to-one narratives. Imagine you've just arrived at a party, which means—unless you want to be left standing in the corner alone—it's crucial to convey a positive, upbeat tone that's sure to engage and delight. And if you ever want to be invited back again, don't be a downer.

- **Keep it short.** Know your social medium platforms and their word count limitations. And whenever possible, stay under the word count. Social media posts aren't the place for pontificating. Think headline, punchline, and CTA.

- **Leverage assets.** The nature of social media platforms and their communities are not shy. Users expect to engage and interact with your content, so don't let them down. Whenever it makes sense and complements the brand strategy, be sure to include a gif, video, infographic, link to full story, or some opportunity to expand their knowledge or curiosity.

- **Always think CTA**: Call to actions go hand-in-hand with brand content, and it's no different in the social media space. In fact, users are socially trained to respond or in some way interact with your content. Don't be shy: Go for the like, share, event invite, video experience, or download. Just don't leave 'em hanging for what to do next.

I encourage you to dive deeper into the fascinating world of social media communications, especially if this is (or becomes) one of your core responsibilities as a brand copywriter. And as you delve deeper into this unique style of copywriting, be mindful of—and keep up with—the ever-evolving dynamics of today's social media platforms so your content stays fresh, relevant, and effective.

PART TEN

COPY THAT EMOTES

EMOTIONAL COPY IS KEY TO READER RESPONSE.

Words have feelings too.

Well, maybe not. But string a few choice ones together and they can bring a reader to tears—or to joy, elation, or an inspired state of mind. That's a fact. Poets, novelists, and authors of great literature over the centuries have mastered the uncanny ability to transform groupings of one-dimensional words into real-life feelings, striking an emotional chord with their readership.

A carefully considered, perfectly appointed arrangement of words can have the power to leap—almost of free will—right off the page (or screen) and into the reader's psyche, triggering a myriad of emotions. In the world of marketing, we want our content to do the same: to animate the reader's imagination to envision the best possible version of themselves and ultimately feel compelled to take action.

As a brand copywriter, you don't have the benefit of leveraging body language or voice inflection to evoke feelings or emotions live, in person. Instead, you need to count on the reader's imagination to engage your words to conjure something deeply felt. No matter what you're writing about, it's important to leverage your intimate knowledge of the target audience to craft emotionally-driven messages that motivate, influence, and persuade them in some way.

It's all about them (not you)

So how do you make the reader—your ideal buyer, persona, target audience—feel something when they read your content? You start by first making the message all about them and how the product or service you're communicating about will improve their lives or transform them in some meaningful way. Your message needs to be deeply authentic, with the single intent of not only identifying their pain point with pinpoint accuracy but offering a solution that solves it.

Naturally, your copy must include the baseline components that are fundamental to a compelling overall message, but once it does, you need to go further. Much further. Your brand copy needs to go beyond the catchy headline, the whizbang features and benefits, and the "call now, operators are standing by with a free toaster" CTA.

Yeah, but why?

The copy formula is in place. You've covered the what, when, where, and how. And you're feeling pretty proud of yourself. But don't stop. Not now. This is where you creatively pause to consider one of the most critical messaging elements of your copy: the why. So, stop. Put down your pen or shut your laptop cover, and back away slowly. It's time to step back, visualize your persona, and intimately reacquaint yourself with their world before you go any further.

- What challenges do they face?
- What keeps them up at night?
- What are their goals?
- What's important to them?
- What are their constraints?

Your message will be completely void of any real value if you don't take time to consider the biggest question on your reader's mind: "Why should I care?"

Be specific. This is not the time or place for empty marketing speak. Your message needs to bring it home. It needs to be personal. You need to directly tie the benefits of the offer to something that will—with absolute clarity—result in an improved personal or professional outcome or state of being. That means no minced words, no marketing vapor, no jargon. You need to make it real. And not just real, but real for the reader.

Your message needs to hit home, then bring it home.

Make 'em feel something, then make 'em do something

To energize your copy so it makes the reader feel something, align the messaging so closely to a very real personal or professional need that it triggers an emotional chord—one that says, "Hey, they get me, they really understand me!" This is an ideal reaction, resulting in a sense of hope and anticipated delight that the offer will deliver a promise-filled solution—one that will transform the reader in some way.

Marketing copy that truly converts prospects to customers appeals to more than the logic. It strikes at a much deeper level and takes emotion-packed, strategically worded language in your copy to get them there. This will significantly improve the likelihood of motivating action.

High emotion words

Words can transform a reader's state of mind from indifference to engagement, or boredom to excitement. There are countless emotionally charged words and phrases that can help trigger just about any feeling or response needed to optimize the value of your brand copy. Here are just a few choice sentiments I've used that can encourage positive emotions and move your reader to action:

- Curiosity
- Empowerment
- Happiness
- Inspiration
- Purpose

- Knowledge
- Belonging
- Value
- Desire
- Time
- Urgency

Emotional copy is the key to reader response. While we may pride ourselves on being highly rational, that's not always how things play out when evaluating the written word. For most of us, you've got to get past the gut and the heart before you can get to the decision-making part of the brain. Just ask anyone who fell in love with a shiny new sports car before considering the cost of maintenance, insurance, and fuel. Or the enthusiastic New Year's–resolution guy who envisions the broad shoulders and six-pack abs but not the amount of space the expensive fitness contraption will take up in his living room.

Your job is to communicate the whole picture, not just part of it, so the reader can enjoy both the emotional and rational satisfaction of making a good decision.

COPY TIP

Sharpen your pencils. Know what your audience wants, then leverage emotionally-driven copy to inspire them to action. Here's how:

- Understand the void that plagues the reader's world.
- Determine the desired action you want them to take (e.g., buy, like, share, attend, download).
- Identify the emotional state that will drive that action (e.g., knowledge, happiness, empowerment).
- Craft copy that creates a vision of their challenge solved or in an ideal state.

PART ELEVEN

A TINY WORD ON MICROCOPY

THEY MAY BE TINY, BUT THEY HAVE A BIG IMPACT.

You don't always need a lot of words to make a big impact, especially when it comes to writing microcopy. Generally reserved for user experience (UX) copywriters, microcopy lives primarily in apps and online retailer websites. They are exactly what you might think: small bits of copy designed to help users do what they need to do and when—quickly, easily, and clearly.

The very nature of their "tininess" makes it particularly challenging for even the most skilled UX copywriters. After all, on average you only have one word—or possibly up to three—to get your point across in a convincing, confident, reassuring manner so that you—and the user—get the desired results.

Some common examples include:

- Continue
- Check in

- Buy now
- Add to cart
- Get updates
- Sign up

Personally, I strongly encourage you to be as creative as the context of what you're writing about will allow. Whenever possible, experiment and A/B test alternative creative microcopy, and above all else, try having a little fun with it. For example:

- I'm ready
- Let's do this
- Make it happen
- See for yourself
- I'm all in
- Sign me up

You get the picture. These targeted, contextual copy bits guide the reader or user through the platform experience and sometimes can include longer copy, like:

- You may want to bookmark this page.
- We need this information because …
- Don't worry, we've emailed you a copy.

- We never sell or share your personal information.
- Your account is all set up. You're good to go!

Never underestimate their might. They may be tiny, but they have a big impact on user experience, and artfully done, can be the defining difference between what customers think are good products and the ones they truly love.

The what-to-do-now copy

Like CTAs, the key to microcopy success is predictability. These power-packed phrases tell the user exactly what to expect—or what not to expect—step by step, encouraging right action that improves their level of confidence along the online journey. And keep in mind, not everyone is a techie. The online or app experience can be an intimidating one depending on your audience, so give 'em a break. Be their thoughtful and courteous guide. Make it easy for them. They'll thank you for it, and so will the techies of the world.

PART TWELVE

GOING DEEP

GO DEEP TO CREATE AUTHENTIC, STRATEGICALLY-DRIVEN COPY.

Just how reliable, dependable, and sustainable is your ability to focus? You owe it to yourself—and your potential as a creative copywriter—to find out.

As a dedicated copywriter, you're constantly learning new things to improve your skills toward mastering the craft. And with all that knowledge and experience, you've gained a solid framework for constructing powerful copy that engages, influences, inspires, and sells. That's good. But mechanics aside—apart from the research, interviews, construction, and copyediting—just how do you get to the actual writing? I mean, how do you really get there—to the heart and soul of the topic at hand?

What's in a word?
I've always had a special relationship with words. Even at a very young age, I knew that words were a powerful form

of communication and as such should be constructed with care, respect, and precision. I've regarded words as mystical arrangements of letters that produce not only sound but meaning, with an intrinsic power to convey a seemingly endless array of emotion and sentiment.

Words, like protons—invisible to the naked eye, but powerful particles of matter—carry the weight of sentiment that can, in an instant, raise the spirits of a fellow human being to inspiring new heights or topple their aspirations in a swift, cutting blow. Fascinating.

An odd thing, I suppose, to be so acutely aware of the power of words at such a young age. But it's that very sensitivity that continues to be the driving force of my creativity today, and my desire to write authentic copy.

Words, the foundation of verbal human communication, are powerful. They have impact. And while our reservoir of vocabulary resides in our conscious thinking, the power to thoughtfully arrange them to deliver authentic meaning resides in a place far deeper in our minds. This place is where I go to find just the right words to express exactly what I wish to convey—and also where I draw inspiration when I want to express myself through art. I imagine it's where everyone flocks when they truly want to tap into their creative potential. It's the place we go where literal meaning fades away, making room for the senses and feelings behind them.

This, for me, is the birthing ground for the creative process—for every truly creative endeavor. And I imagine it is for you, too. The trick is getting there, to that place where authenticity reigns, every time you wish to create customer value-driven copy.

Know your process

Whatever your process is for going deep into that creative place, honor it. The path or process is likely different for everyone, but the result is the same. You get there. And you know it because time melts away, giving way to a surge of ideas that seem endless.

You're drawn to it. And you want to remain in that magically creative place as long as you possibly can until something, someone—or mental exhaustion—draws you out. At least until the next time.

> It feels good. Heck, it feels great because you know you've arrived at the place where authenticity reigns. Like waterfalls of inspiration, you're suddenly the unlikely bucket scooping from the furious flow of ideas as fast as you can because you simply don't want to miss a drop.

You know when you've arrived where authenticity reigns.

Every writer's process is different. The important thing is to know yours. For me, it starts with removing the literal and figurative clutter from my to-do list of the day—and any visual clutter there may be on my desk—freeing my mind to focus on the assignment at hand. I then shut down my smart phone and all smart devices—no email checking, no distracting news feeds, and above all, no social media. These are killers of time, attention, and precious energy. Once I've set the groundwork, then comes the critical choice of music to set just the right mood. I prefer movie scores—I love them. The musical notes play in the background like a soundtrack to my inward adventure to the creative depths of my mind. It works like magic every time.

The goal is to create an environment conducive for sustaining uninterrupted blocks of deep thought, which for me ranges from around two to four hours. This range may be different for you. But for me, that's about my daily limit for engaging in truly deep thought.

As rewarding as the process is, it can be exhausting. And it's then, immediately following these hours-long bouts of creative flow, that the best thing I can do is get out of my head and back into the world to get reenergized. For me it's the gym or, at the very least, a long but brisk walk. Pick your poison: a swim, run, or game of tennis. Whatever it is that effectively gets you out of your head and into something physical that you enjoy doing.

This is also a great technique for combatting writer's block. This physical distraction not only reenergizes but also provides an easy way to discover inspiration, get new ideas, and jumpstart your creative flow. For me, when I redirect my energy from mental to physical activity, my mind relaxes then fires with new ways and ideas to tackle the assignment or inspires a whole new or even better direction. Works for me every time.

If you want better results from your copywriting, practice optimizing your time and attention so you can hone your ability to go deep. Really deep. This means prioritizing the time you put aside to research, write, and create by abandoning the distractions of the day, which helps you pave the way to your creative place. These critical preparatory steps—whatever they are for you—allow you to break through the superficial surface of the writing process and plunge unapologetically inward and upward to the good stuff.

A FINAL WORD ON WORDS

Get your head around it

As we come to a close, you've likely noticed that this book is premised primarily on my personal philosophy, influenced by real-world experience and messaging approaches that have worked for me. It's not a how-to book or a technical manual on crafting brand narrative supported by university studies and research findings. There are plenty of wonderfully informative books out there that address the technical side of messaging and how they can help hone and expand your writing capabilities. Equally, there are many exciting facets to learn about in the world of marketing copywriting, and I encourage you to explore them all.

This book, however, is simply one copywriter's take on, well, what it takes to boost your writing ability from good to great by way of a mind-set—by diving much deeper into the discovery process about a brand. It's the kind of creative thought approach that goes beyond topical features and benefits, and reaches intrepidly for the core truth about the brand promise. It's about getting your head wrapped around the brand essence, then tethering its truth to an authentic narrative that draws a clear connection between the mechanics of a brand's offering and what's really in it for the targeted reader: the experience.

Clients and accountants and copywriters—oh my

My clients are smart. Most are. They're either proud and accomplished founders of their businesses, or they hold prominent executive roles in their organizations, responsible for the development and promotion of their flagship products. And when it comes to marketing, they know exactly what they want—a print, digital, or web marketing asset that exudes the features and benefits of their offering presented in a way that's informative, engaging, and relevant.

But not every executive is good at everything. It's just not reasonable to expect, nor do they have the bandwidth. While they hold a clear vision of a marketing roadmap for successfully launching their products, they may not always know how to pull it all together from a messaging standpoint—that is, corralling the precise words and sentiment needed to create a unique value proposition or crafting strategic messaging that will distinctly position their products in the marketplace.

I liken this experience to me and accounting. Stay with me.

Sure. I'm good with numbers. I can balance a checkbook and file my own taxes. But, frankly, it makes my head hurt. And I don't have the time (or the interest) to be a pro at everything. When it comes to doing taxes, I hire a professional. They're smart, experienced, talented folks who are capable of delivering exactly what I need. And they actually enjoy it.

This is what I believe our clients think about brand copywriters. Sure, they're smart, intelligent professionals who could craft a story if they really needed to. But, like me with accounting, it likely makes their heads hurt to think about—or it just doesn't make sense to attempt being a pro at every marketing discipline. So, they reach out to a knowledgeable, skilled copywriter who is capable and experienced and actually enjoys the process of storytelling.

That's you.

My point being: Know that when a client reaches out to you for brand messaging support, it's a privilege, not an entitlement. Never take for granted that they chose you to help them champion and nurture their brand endeavors. After all, they're entrusting you with one of the most critical differentiators in an increasingly competitive marketplace—a brand and its story.

So, accept each copywriting mission humbly, go all in, and—most importantly—deliver with unwavering authenticity. Always.

www.ingramcontent.com/pod-product-compliance
Lightning Source LLC
Chambersburg PA
CBHW030818180526
45163CB00003B/1333